Let's Take a Walk on the Wild Side and Other Silly Verse

by

Roger Ling

 New Generation Publishing

THE STORY SO FAR

The following words are the story of country boy born out in the sticks in a farm cottage a mile from our nearest neighbor's in 1948. I had a fantastic childhood even though until I was 11 we had a pump in the garden for our water, an outside bucket and chuck it 18 steps from the back door (14 steps in the dark), that my dad had to empty into the bumby hole, and no electricity, gas, or phone. Whenever dad dug a new bumby hole, he would plant his rhubarb over the one he had just filed in, mum's rhubarb pies were quite famous. Most of what I have written happened or didn't happen in the village near Chelmsford in Essex where I grew up, the stories are in no particular order. Slurpy Jack and Storky Crane, both entirely fictitious characters were both famous liars, but people would come from miles around to sit round the fire in the public bar of the pub, to listen to tales of the latest exploits of Mrs Day or Big Bren and the vicar. This is a collection of silly verse and anecdotes mainly written long before political correctness became an issue, so if you are likely to be offended please read no further.

I was thirteen in 1961 for me the start of the swinging sixties, our village had a brilliant youth club held in a hut on the football ground, where we learned to do the twist and to jive, to the latest pop songs, it was a time when a band was called a group and they actually played instruments. At that time every village hall held a "dance" about once a month and it was a chance to meet girls and maybe get close enough to actually touch one, on the pretence of wanting to dance. The event was usually run by the scout master, or the local vicar or a school teacher trying to be hip, none of whom had a clue what us teenagers wanted in the way of music. The disco was a thing of the future; we had a Grundig record player and a few 45 R.P.M records that got played over and over again. The local group would usually play, some of them would have homemade instruments, like a double bass made from a tea chest a broom stick and some string or mothers wash board and a few thimbles made a brilliant percussion section. The music was bad but it was loud and we loved it.

The best looking girls were always with the band and sat like trophies at the front table, screeching and singing along. The boys stood by the bar drinking coke or lemonade trying to look cool, the smell of brilliantine was over powering and even overpowered the smell of sweat. Deodorant for men was for pansies and ladies' hairdressers. The girls sat on the other side of the room trying to look disinterested in the boys and smelling of lavender, talking behind their hands and laughing, it was a brave teenager that took that walk across the floor for the first time, knowing if she said yes the other lads would cheer, but if she said no they would jeer. The first poem is about the first time I got jeered. In common with most young men much of my energy was used up in the pursuit of girls, this led to many rejections all of them making the next one just a little bit easier.

THE LONGEST WALK

Do you remember going to dances?
When you were in your teens,
With your hair slicked back with brilliantine
And wearing your fancy jeans.

The lads all stood on one side,
The girls stood on the other.
And there was always a really gorgeous one
With a friend like Godzilla's mother.

So you'd toss a coin with one of your mates,
To see who would ask who to dance.
And the older lads always moved in,
Before you got the chance.

Then you'd see one you really fancied,
And try hard to catch her eye.
In the hope she'd show she was interested,
Before you give it a try.

Then you'd take the longest walk of your life,
Across the dance hall floor.
And panic in case she could smell you,
As you sweat from every pore

And the talc that you'd poured down your Y fronts
Would escape with the speed of a snail.
And you could feel the whole room watching,
As you left a little white trail.

And you'd walk up to the one that you'd chosen,
And ask coolly do you want a dance.
And she'd laugh and say very loudly,
Clear off sonny, no chance.

And you'd hope the floor would split open,
And you'd disappear in the crack.
You'd hide the hurt as you walk to your own side.
Leaving footprints in your own track.

You had to put on a brave front
Though you wanted to run away
But it helped you understand
Why some of your mates turned gay

Living where we did out in the sticks, we were fairly sheltered from what was happening in the wide world, right up until we went to secondary school.

That was the time you started to notice girls (some of them had breasts which I found very attractive). I was lucky in that I had a brother eighteen months older than me who helped me through the hard parts and later took me into Chelmsford to the cool places where the mods hung out.

When I was about 14 a girl friend from the village cut my hair in a Beatle cut and restyled my jacket so it had no collar just like the fab four. My mum was not impressed

School uniform was just for the high school and the posh kids, so I went to school with my new look and it changed my last year at school instantly, girls liked me and even the school bully no longer wanted to beat me up.

JACK THE LAD

During the nineteen sixties
When sex was first invented
There wasn't that many ways
For babies to be prevented

They had them horrible rubber things
That never were that good
But you couldn't buy them in all the shops
You had to get them where you could

So you would take your chance down at Boots
That some old biddy wouldn't serve
And right at the last minute
I would always lose my nerve

I'd buy a brand new tooth brush
Or a jar of brilliantine
But when I got home
My mum knew where I'd been

So you would go down to the barber's shop
And sit in his big chair
And talk to him about cricket
While he cut your hair

Then he would lean across your shoulder
Like he was your oldest friend
And whisper very quietly
Would you like anything for the weekend

So you would give him your three and nine
And five bob for your hair
You would only buy one packet
More you didn't dare

In case he thought you were a pervert
And went and told your dad
It wasn't much fun in the sixties
Being Jack the lad

Everyone was getting free love
Least everyone but me
But I still went out every Saturday night
With my little packet of three

It was a packet of two really
Because you had to throw one away
So your mates never suspected
That you hadn't had a lay

And we took these purple tablets
That made you lose your head
And never listened to your parents
No matter what they said

And we used to wear fantastic clothes
And a stupid blue beat hat
And be right rude to policemen
And act just like a Pratt

We would hitch hike down to Brighton
And stay up all the night
And stir up the Mods and Rockers
And watch the buggers fight

Then you had to get married
Because your bird was up the duff
I was glad of the excuse to settle down
I recon I'd had enough.

I was 14 in 1962 and was at secondary school coming to the end of my undistinguished academic career it was a time when if you were good at the main subjects you were put in the upper class. The classes went from lower 1 up to upper 1 and so on through until the 4th year. I was in lower middle 1-2 -3 then 4.

You knew exactly where you stood in the education league, and no attempt was made to make you feel better about yourself you were below average and that was it.

But girls and music were my priority and all that school crap just got in the way of having fun, The Beatles and the rolling stones were releasing fantastic sounds and Tamla Mowtown was creeping across the Atlantic and I just wanted to go clubbing with my older brother.

All of the below average boys in my class were recommended by the careers master (who only came to us once) that we should try to get apprenticeships as painter & decorators, Middle 4 were recommended to be plumbers, upper middle 4 electricians & mechanics, upper 4 architects or draughtsmen. The girls in my class got jobs in Woolworths or one of the local cafes.

I was sent for an interview with an old family builder in Chelmsford and at that time if you could hold a paint brush you would automatically get the job. I was still only 14 when I left school and it was like being released from prison. When I was 15 radio Caroline came on air off the Essex coast and music I didn't know existed was everywhere

James Brown, Otis Reading, Wilson Picket, etc. 1964 was a fantastic year for a teenager living in Chelmsford. The corn exchange was one of the best music venues in the U.K. The Who, Georgie Fame, Jimmy Hendrix, Rufus Thomas, Zoot Money, were just a few of the big names that would come to our small town and blew us away.

I earned about three pounds a week. Mum took ten shillings for my keep a packet of twenty cigarettes cost two shillings and six pence. It was less than ten bob to get in the corn exchange and ten French blues cost ten bob.

We usually left the corn exchange a few minutes before closing time at midnight, so we could run the few hundred yards to the railway station to catch the six minutes past twelve train to Liverpool street. Just after midnight we would buy a platform ticket from the machine for a penny it would have Sundays date on it. The six minutes past twelve train was a slow one that stopped at every station and had no ticket collector which was good as we had no ticket. At Stratford station the main line train stopped one side of the platform and the underground stopped at the other so it was easy to jump on the tube and get off at Piccadilly.

The clubs were everywhere The Markey, The Flamingo, The Scène, The Last chance saloon, to name just a few, they all sold just soft drinks and sometimes ice lolly's as none of them had any windows and it could get a bit hot dancing the night away.

Home on the first train showing the platform ticket at the barrier.

I don't recommend anyone tries our method of travel now but in the sixties it seemed natural thing to do. We were lucky enough to see Muddy Waters and many other American blues stars perform at the Fairfield hall in Croydon another small venue where you were close enough to touch them.

We were very privileged to have been around at that time no other generation will ever be that lucky.

THREE WEDDINGS AND A SPUTNIK

We avoided the cracks in the pavement

Like you do on a Saturday night

And my pockets were full of plasters

In case I got in a fight

And there was trouble over in Cuba

Between the Russians and the Yanks

All the pictures on the telly

Were of guided missiles and tanks

I think I went to a wedding

And stuffed something up my nose

Nuclear war worried me as much

As having the latest clothes

James brown was on the duke box

Otis Reading wasn't quite dead

We stayed up all night taking tablets

And strange things went on in my head

President Kennedy got himself murdered

By some nutter or the F. B. I

We worried about all them sputniks

The Russians put up in the sky

There was trouble over in Vietnam

And people were making a fuss

Cassius Clay won at the boxing

But that didn't bother us

I went to another wedding

I don't think I ever knew where

And me mates were dropping like ninepins

But I was too busy to care

Luther King was still making noises

Till they shot him one day in the park

And the summer just went on for ever

And it always seemed to be dark

Then I went to another wedding

They all said I'd be fine

It wasn't quite the same as the others

I think it must have been mine

It brought that day to a sudden end

Or perhaps it was more than a year

Or maybe it didn't happen to me

Isn't the memory queer.

In our small village there was three shops plus two butchers and two pubs in a small village with a population of less than one thousand people in the 1950s, one was a general store one was a sweet shop that also sold bicycles and spares such as tyre's inner tubes etc. the smell of rubber was overpowering, we had no electricity in our house so we used a wireless that needed accumulator's as a source of power, as I got bigger one of my jobs was to carry the two heavy glass accumulators over a mile to the bike shop to be charged up, so we could listen to the goons and the archers how times have changed.

THE SHOP

I had to walk to Mrs. Barnies
To get mums weekly shop
She never had much money
So it never was a lot

There was a chair in front of the counter
For the fat old ladies to sit
And to a lad of ten years' old
They were always talking shit

The old ladies smelt of moth balls
And the old men smelt of wee
But she always used to serve them first
If they came in after me.

Children had to know their place
And be seen and never heard
Some old folks would treat you like crap
And you dare not say a word

I never minded
Standing to wait my turn
I liked to hear the gossip
It's amazing what you could learn

There was the smell of fresh ground coffee
And brawn and butter and lard
The eggs were still warm from the chicken's bum
That She kept out in the yard

You could get a bag of sweets for a penny
And sometimes she would sell you one fag
And after she'd cut your bacon
She wiped her hands on an old greasy rag

My kids go to the supermarket
Where everything smells the same
There's no danger you may get poisoned
And I think it's a bloody shame

I never quite understood the Japanese attitude to aphrodisiacs but I never understood Japanese.

I read in the paper the other day

About these Africans that get up at dawn

And go out and shoot a rhino

So a Japanese can have the horn

LET'S TAKE A WALK ON THE WILD SIDE

I like to walk on the wild side every now and then,
so I sit up and watch channel four till way past half
past ten
or I'll look at the naked ladies in the Sunday sport
or drive without a seat belt and don't care if I get
caught.

I'll go into a bookie's and gamble away a pound
I'll eat an entire mars bar and throw the wrapper on
the ground
I eat the fat off me bacon and putt's sugar in me tea
All that shit the doctors say never bothers me.

Once just for the hell of it I 'ad sex all on me own
or answer back the missus, or eat beef straight off
the bone
I nearly plucked up courage once to talk dirty to
the wife
I've become a proper rebel in my latter life.

I bought myself a motor bike and all the biker gear
It will never pass the MOT so it wasn't very dear
When I put me leathers on I look a proper toff
And I rev my engine really loud to piss the
neighbors off

Sometimes in the winter I go out without a vest
I'm thinking of 'having Madonna tattooed on me
chest
I'm completely out of control that's how it seems
to me
so I have another happy pill and nice hot cup of tea.

LONDONERS

We get lots of people from London round here
And they always call you John
We put up with during the summer
But we are bloody glad when they've gone

THE WONDER OF POO

Isn't dog shit wonderful stuff
It just lay in your path and don't smell
Till you tread it in to the carpet
Then it stinks like hell.

MY DOG HAS A DOG'S LIFE

My old dog has nothing to do
Except plan where is the best place to crap
So some unsuspecting person
Will tread in his smelly trap.

SOMETHING ELSE I DON'T UNDERSTAND

Why do dogs smell each other's bums?

Is it some sort of game they play?

If it wasn't for sleeping and eating

My dog would do it all day.

A survey by one of the red top papers came up with the opinion that gay couples make the best parents.

RECENT NEWS

They say lesbians make good parents,

I don't know how they knows

But I know from personal experience

They make bloody good videos

THE LADY WITH THE GOOD COMPLEXION

She said I got skin like a babies bum,
Why don't you kiss it and see?
So I did, and she were right,
It was damp and tasted of wee.

OR IF YOU PREFER

I got skin like a babies bum she said
Why don't you give it a kiss?
So I did and she was right
It was damp and tasted of piss.

BITCH

Life's a bitch they say
Well that isn't fair on life
If you want to know what's a bitch
You ought to meet my wife

A FARMER'S DELIGHT

They turned one of our barns in to a pub

And it tickles me a bit

To see them posh folks eating

Where my bullocks used to shit

© G. PARKINSON '98

MANURE

Horse manure one pound a bag

It said on a gate near us

Dad dumped them off a trailer load

They didn't half make a fuss

The next little ditty came into my head in a flow of words that even to this day I can't explain. I wrote it on a piece of paper all the way through in a matter of minutes without a pause, and when I came to type it onto my P.C it did not require any changes, apart from spelling mistakes. I am not aware of knowing a young man called Frank with a wife with small breasts.

This poem, as with many of them, was written when we were in the pub in Suffolk, and I have to admit that breasts were quite often the main topic of conversation in the public bar, especially when the yuppies were in.

For those of my readers that don't know, yuppies stood for Young, Upwardly mobile professional people. Lots of villages were populated by the young professionals, in the late 80's and 90's as property prices rose the young locals could no longer afford to live in the more picturesque villages and the Yuppies moved in. This was resented by a few but most people accepted the fact that if the village shop and pub were to survive we needed them, they were mostly very nice people and they brought some good looking women to the pub and much needed revenue to the village.

FRANKS LITTLE PROBLEM

Young Franks wife always made the effort
To try and look her best
But Frank were quite dissatisfied
With her nonexistent breasts

I can't say I ever noticed
I don't look at things like that
But once he said it, I made it my business
And he was right she were completely flat

We were discussing his little problem
In the pub just like you do
And we decided we should help him
After we'd had a few

We decided on silicone implants
But frank didn't have no cash
But old Jim the taxidermist
Said he would have a bash

So we'd got ourselves a surgeon
But we had no silicone
Mr. Hall what worked for the gas board
Said he'd got some at home

So an anesthetic was needed
And just then young Mickey Finn
Reckoned he had got something
We could slip in to her gin

Young frank was so excited
He couldn't wait to tell is wife
He reckoned it was the present
She'd wanted all her life

Mr. Hall went to get his silicone
Old Jim went to get his knife
And young frank was so excited
He ran to get his wife

We cleared the kitchen table
And cut up some old sheets
We'd seen that on the telly
On the cow boy film repeats

We boiled up lots of water
All in preparation
And the lads settled down with a pint
To watch the operation

Mr. Hall came back with his silicone
But we hadn't got no molds
So we hunted round the kitchen
And found some pudding bowls

Young Frank came back at midnight
said is wife wouldn't come
we thought that right ungrateful
After all that we had done

Franks wife don't let him out now
And I think that's bloody unkind
But I keep's her breasts behind the bar
In case she changes her mind

The local's all settled down to watch the operation.

A NEW ONE

I wrote this poem about Deja vu
Why I'm really not sure
Then I suddenly got this feeling
I'd written it once before

A NEW ONE

I wrote this poem about Deja vu
Why I'm really not sure
Then I suddenly got this feeling
I'd written it once before

THE DISADVANTAGE OF DRINK

My wife's trying to stop me drinking
I find that a little bit queer
I wouldn't have married her in the first place
If I hadn't had too much beer

WRONG DIAGNOSIS

Big Bren went to the doctors
With pain's in her arms and her chest
We put it down to strain
From the weight of them gigantic breasts

The Doc said she got acute angina
Well that I'd like to dispute
I seen it dozens of times
And I'd hardly call it cute.

CLOSE SHAVE

I caught my wife using my razor
I normally wouldn't care
The hair off her chest were bad enough
I draw the line at pubic hair

CLOSE ENCOUNTER OF THE
ABSURD KIND

Our eyes met across a crowded room,
Not a word was said,
There was this incredible look, that said, I'm
yours take me to bed.
A sexy nod of the head,
A cheeky wink of the eye,
The sound of heavy breathing,
The sensual rub of the thigh
The moment was electric
No one could resist
But the look she gave me back
Said clear off moron your pissed

I DO LIKE TO BE BESIDE THE SEA SIDE

Come to Frinton they said

For the company and sea air

Well the air smelt just like Chelmsford

And I was the only bugger there

I LIKE IT HERE

You know how you lays awake at night

Worrying about them Japanese

And are the Swiss trying to rule the world

With the mold they puts in their cheese

And you can't drink the water

Cos they puts that fluoride in

So you worries about the cost

Of cleaning your teeth with gin

And you has to burn your rubbish

So the bin men don't know what you've had

And you like to wear the vest

You've had since you were a lad

And you have to put salt in your shoes

Every Sunday afternoon

And you turns round the table cloth

When it happens to be full moon

And you keep forgetting your wife's name

Though you've had the same one for years

And you're frightened to go into Chelmsford

Cos it always ends in tears

And you realize that your only friend

Is your next door neighbor's cat

And the Samaritans tell you to bugger off

When you phone up for a chat

And your teeth itch all the time

And there's voices in your head

And you have a conversation

And forget everything you said.

Well you should tell it to your doctor

I did the other day

They was going to send me home next week

Now they've said I can stay.

A TRIP TO THE FAR NORTH

I spent a month in Blackpool one weekend
And it rained the whole dam time
And there were all these yuppies from Liverpool
Drinking lager and lime

The beer tasted like gnat's piss
And the chips all tasted of fat
And I don't think they let you live in the north
Unless you're a total prat
And the women all had curlers in
And so did some of the men
And the pubs all had beer on the floor
And closed at half past ten

The wind blew sharp sand in your face
If you dared to walk on the pier
And there were policemen in every doorway
Huddled together in fear

There were drunken Scotsmen everywhere
Trying to start a fight
You only went out in the day time
You daren't go out at night

There was so much noise you couldn't hear
yourself think
And there were a smell of fried fish in the air
And if you wanted to go and sit on the beach
They charged you a quid for a chair

Well I've always wanted to travel the world
And see what other folks did
But you won't make me leave Essex again
Not even for a million quid.

IS NORFOLK IN THE NORTH?

My sister went to Yarmouth
Nice enough place she said
Sept most of the youngster was hooligans
And most of the old folks were dead

THE DIRTY WOMAN

I once went with a dirty woman
Gave her all my cash
She gave me a bloody good time
And a horrible embarrassing rash

THE DINNER PARTY

I aint ever gone much on eating,
What with living in a pub,
But some posh folks from the village
Invited me round for grub,
Of course I 'ad to eat it
Well I 'aren't one to be rude,
But no wonder their women are skinny
If that's what they call food

GERMANS

Have you ever seen one of them Germans Naked?

No nor aint I

I often wonder what they look like

Then I wonder-----Why?

© G. PARKINSON '08

(Naked German?)

WE ARE ON OUR OWN

If I'd been one o' them lesbians
Or a homosexual come to that
Or I was an ethnic minority
Anorexic or excessively fat
Or if I was a single mother
Or had spent some time in jail
Or was one of them unfortunate fellows
Who can't decide if they are male
Or if I'd done a murder
Or never new me dad
Or had a history in me family
Of going raving mad
Or if I'd never had a job
Or done a full day's work
And spent all my time at school
Learning how to shirk
Or if I'd still got aids
Or it came back again
Or had a wart on me nose
Or water on the brain
Or if I was a wino

Or lived out on the street
Or even if I was stupid
Or had bigger than average feet
Or if I was a junky
Or gambled to excess
Or if I was a weirdo
And liked to wear a dress
No matter what my problem
Or how low I stoop
I could look through the yellow pages
And find a supportive group
There's a support group for prostitutes
Pimps whores and tarts
And I know because my dad goes
There's one for boring farts
There's a support group for the clergy
For lords and all their heirs
But there's one section of humanity
Where no one really cares
Us ordinary blokes what lead ordinary lives
Live in ordinary houses with ordinary wives
We do ordinary jobs for ordinary pay

There aint no group to support us and help us through the day

So I decided to set one up

Form a sort of club

Then it struck me that we'd got one

It's called the local pub

UNNATURAL DISASTER

There was a flood in South America
She watched it on T.V.
Thousands of people killed
And their homes washed out to sea.

She reached for the remote control
And flicked to the other side
There were the bodies of little children
Caught up in genocide.

She changed channels again
There weren't no men
Just women and children and flies
In their eyes

Paul O'Grady was on the B.B.C.
With a cat with a boil on its neck
She reached into her handbag
And wrote him out a cheque.

ANOTHER WET DREAM

I used to have wet dreams about them spice girls

But I must be getting old

Women don't cause my wet dreams these days

Its lack of bladder control

<u>Rose spice</u>

42

In the village where we once lived was a beautiful lady called Rowena who doted on both her horse and her dog, (I'm sure she doted on her husband too though that wasn't quite so apparent) Her horse was the envy of most of the men that knew her, this poem is the result.

ROWENA

I been having this dream just lately
And it's hard to get out me head
There's times when it worries me
So I'm scared to go to bed.

I dream I'm on all fours
Grazing grass out in the sun
And I'm always completely stark naked
With just a tail to cover me bum

Then this beautiful woman appears
And looks into my eyes
Then she climbs on to my back
And grips me between her thighs

Then she strokes my neck
And blows gently in my ear
And I know that I'm in love
And it's mutual that's quite clear.

Then she leads me to a quiet spot
And lays me down in some hay
She lets me nuzzle me nose between her breasts
And there she lets me stay

It's just a silly fantasy
Just a dream of course
But no one could have a better life
Than the lovely Rowena's horse.

O Rowena, Rowena, Rowena,
You'd understand if you'd ever seen her
It's only a dream of course
But I'd love to be her horse.

THE BARMAIDS APRON

I was sniffing the barmaid's apron
Like a land lord has to do
When the wife came in and caught me
Christ did the air turn blue

She called me a dirty bastard
And her a filthy whore
And threw her out there and then
Said don't come back no more.

I convinced her it was part of a land lords job
And we were having a laugh and joke
But she sacked the barmaid any way
And employed an ugly bloke.

FRANK'S NEW BUSINESS

He read in the daily telegraph
about this woman who wanted a kid
and bought some sperm from America
and paid two thousand quid

So the hero of our story
by the way his name was Frank
reckoned he could do that
So he set up a sperm bank

He went down to the dump
and brought some bottles home
and set about to fill them
while he was on his own

When he'd got enough
He thought he'd make a start
so he put a four-line advert
in the new exchange and mart

It said is anybody interested
White heterosexual male
plays allot of cricket
and has got some sperm for sale

Well he didn't get a phone call
not a single one
but he carried on filling the bottles
Cos he said that it was fun

Well it all was pretty harmless
least that's ow it seemed to me
till is mum got a bottle out the fridge
and nearly put it in her tea

he's a lorry driver now
I've seen him in his tanker
I don't know how he got that job
He was a merchant banker

Franks new business

THE MOUSE

We had this mouse loose in our parlor
Covering the place with crap
The wife didn't want to hurt it
So we bought a humane trap
Well we set it with some chocolate
And caught it just like that
It didn't feel a bloody thing
Till I fed it to the cat

A MYSTERY SOLVED

I bought some Chinese food
Off this Chinese chap
Now I know why they all look ill
They don't half eat some crap

As a landlord it was part of my job to get a bit tipsy, and talk rubbish with the locals, this next load of rubbish was the result of a serious conversation had between a few of us in the early hours of the morning after much Irish whisky had been consumed, (if we were in for an evening of talking crap Irish whisky was the safest tipple to keep everyone in good humor, Scotch on the other hand could have disastrous consequences)

HOW MRS DAY PREVENTED BIOLOGICAL WARFARE IN THE MIDDLE EAST WITH THE AID OF A DUSTPAN IN BRACKETS AND NO BRUSH

There was this rumor going round about Mrs. Day
Well there aint no smoke without fire
But I heard it from old Storky crane
Who was famous for being a liar

She was having it off so he said
With a chap who were a brush millionaire
He lived in the posh part of Brentwood
Where a leg over's called an affair

He made his money selling dustpans
During the war with Iraq
And so he didn't break no sanctions
He held all the hand brushes back

So old Saddam issued a fatwa
No one here knew what that were
Mrs. Day were a bit on the big side
So she thought he'd aimed it at her

Well, it so happened she had once slept with a
solder
Who most of the time wasn't mad
And he had been with a haw out in Thailand
Who'd been housekeeper for old Saddams dad

Now then
Saddams dad had three gold teeth
Installed by a dentist in Bow
And he'd been paid with some shares in an oil well
And the war were stopping the flow

Now hears the nub of the story
Out in Texas they'd had an oil rush
And the haw that lived out in Thailand
Had a dustpan that dint have no brush

Now the S.A.S was recruiting
And some of the lads from round hear
Recon that dressed as a hand brush salesman
They could get Saddam out in a year

It gets complicated now
Storky Crane knew old Saddams mother
He were out there in the Great War
And they swapped the occasional E mail
And of course he'd mentioned the haw

On top of that; Mrs. Day had a gold pendant
Made from Saddams dads teeth
And it were stamped made in Thailand
And Kilroy was here underneath

We never worked out all the connections
But you must know how rumors persist
And we never got the full story
By then old Storky were pissed

AN INTERESTING HOBBY

Since I've reached a certain age
And don't chase women any more
I've developed quite an interest
In my Black and Decker saw

I've joined the Saffron Walden branch
Of the national power saw club
And we has a weekly meeting
And it's always in the pub

We have races cutting chip board
Which we then turn into stools
Then we all sits round a table
And polish up our tools

We don't always wear our anoraks
Sometimes we dress up posh
And invite along a speaker
From Philips or from bosh

You can always tell our members
Cos they've got some fingers short
And were trying to get jig saw driving
As a new Olympic sport

We have in depth conversations
About the merits of each blade
And marvel at the engineering
Of how each machine is made

Since I joined the circular saw club
My wife's gone soft in the head
She keep ranting and winging and raging
About the saw dust she finds in the bed.

She says it's quite unnatural
To be so obsessed with our tools
And refers to the other members
As that bunch of sad old fools.

She says I love my saw
More than I ever did her
And its time for me to choose
Which one I prefer.

Well my saw can't cook me dinner
Iron my shirts, darn my socks, or stitch,
But at least I can stop its constant whine
With the simple flick of a switch.

WASTE O MONEY

I bought my wife some o that face cream
Like the adverts said I should
It'll make her young and beautiful they say
Bloody stuffs no good

ADVENTURE IN CHELMSFORD

I went into Chelmsford on business
Pay me electric and stuff like that
And I met this lovely young lady
And of course we started to chat

She says would you like to do business
I say of course my dear
I've biked all the way into Chelmsford
Why else do you think I'd be here?

She say follow me for a nice cup of tea
And we will talk about a price
Well I were feeling quite thirsty
So I say yes that would be nice

When I'd drunk me tea
She sat on me knee and said its only five pounds
for the lot
I say you can't fool me five pounds, for cold tea
Its two shillings at home, and it's hot

FRANK'S NEW WIFE

Young Frank's wife had left him
After the breast implant affair
'He got home from work one night
And there she was, not there.

Well he was quite upset
She wasn't there to cook 'is grub,
But at least he had his freedom
To come down to the pub.

But it was clear he wasn't happy
Without a woman in his life,
So we decided we should help him
To find another wife.

He deserved to get a good one
After the last one he had had,
So we had a meeting in the pub
To write him out an ad'.

She would have to be good looking
Nothing but the best,
Legs rite up to her bum
And a forty two inch chest.

She would have to be a blonde
There weren't no decent there,
And we thought it might be nice
If she had ginger pubic hair.

We decided on tea total
And she'd have to own a car,
So she could take us to the darts match
And we could have a jar.

She would have to be a good cook
And hardly ever speak,
And not be one to make Frank do sex
More than once a week

.

We sent the advert off
Without any more ado,
And elected a committee
To conduct the interview.

It cost a fiver for the ad'
And much to our surprise,
After all the effort we put in
We didn't get no replies.

A GOOD EXCUSE

I went into town the other day
And there was loads of them wino's there
And they all had two things in common
Wild eyes and a good head of hair

Now you probably never noticed
Cos you always look down on the ground
But you have a look at their lovely hair
Next time you go into town

Now I've always been follicle challenged
And I like to have a few
So I've taken to drinking strong cider
And bottles of special brew

So if you hear me slurring me words
Or see me fall off me chair
It's not cos I want to get pissed
I'm just trying to grow back me hair

I only drink for the sake of me follicles

UNNATURAL ESCAPE

I had one escape from reality
That used to be my dreams
To drift away to that subconscious world
Where nothings what it seems

Lots of dreams I remember
And some I am pleased to forget
Some of them were scary
And some of them were wet

Then I caught insomnia
And found I couldn't sleep
It were my doctor that suggested
I should take up counting sheep.

Well it seemed to work at first
I'd nod off when I'd counted a few
But in my dream I fell in love
With this sexy little yew.

We would graze the grass together
And do other sheep like pursuits
And do disturbing things
Involving Wellington boots.

I decided to become a shepherd
Bought a dog a crook and a hat
But walking the streets of Chelmsford
I felt a proper prat.

My insomnia soon came back
I were scared to go to sleep
I knew as soon as I closed my eyes
Id dream of bloody sheep.

Occasionally when I'm awake
I think of my sexy yew
And I sometimes write her a love song
When I had had a few.

But I think I'm quite cured now
My obsession has run its course
I had her again in my dream last night
But this time with mint sauce.

LATE NIGHT VISITORS

When the moths come taping on the window

For me to let them in to the light

I don't think it would be humane

To lock them out all night

So I open up the fanlight

And welcome them inside

They are the only friend I got

So I aint got no pride.

And as they flutter round the room

Oh so happily

I think it must be fun for them

And its company for me

DON'T IT MAKE YOU WANT TO SPIT?

I used to get real angry, now I just keep calm

I tells myself they can't help it and they don't mean no harm

It's not 'cos they are morons though that's how they appear

They probably got things on their mind and their brains aint in gear

Then they cuts you up on roundabouts and as to blow there horn

But before you can smack em one the buggers are always go'rn

But--I don't get angry I takes it in my stride

I aint going to let them wind me up I got too much pride.

Then your queue up at the check-out that says ten items no more

And there's this bloody woman who's bought up half the store

But-- I don't let them get to me, I'm far too smart for that.

I just acts quite normal cool just like a cat.

Then there's this old man in front of you in a stupid pork pie hat
Taking up all the road and driving like a prat.

But--I just smile and don't bother I just look the other way,

I aint going to let the bastards spoil my peaceful day.

Then this spotty little bar steward who pretends that he can't hear
Chatting up his girlfriend while I'm gasping for a beer.

But--I lay back, keep calm, and always act polite
I won't let the buggers make me start a fight.

Then the wife wants me to talk to her, while there's football on T.V
but when she pretends to be asleep, she won't talk to me

But--that's all right I just let it pass over me head
I could get bloody angry but I smile or laugh instead.

Then your minding your own business and this bloody stupid cow.
I can't say no more, I'm bloody angry now.

I was talking one day around the time Nelson Mandela was released, to a chap called David (probably in a pub) and he was lamenting the loss of his beloved teddy boy suit and telling me how good he thought he looked in it. That conversation about something that happened to a complete stranger 30 years earlier was converted in my head into the following poem.

DAVID AND HIS AMAZING ZOOT SUIT.

I looked really 'hard in my Teddy boy suit
But my mum revealed one day
After I'd kept it for thirty years
She'd given the dam thing away.

She'd give it to bloody Oxfam
I went really mad at 'her
Oxfam I ask 'you'
I don't suppose they knew what it were

I used to stroke its velvet collar
And marvel at the length of the coat
Just thinking about them drain pipe trousers
Brings a lump to my throat.

My steel comb was still in the pocket
I'd sharpened it all down one side
And me shades that I'd nicked out of Woolworth's
That I used to wear with such pride.

And inside the waistcoat pocket
Tucked were me mother couldn't see
Was a picture of the lovely Jane Russell
And a partly used packet of three.

I looked bloody 'hard in that zoot suit
As I strutted round town every night
Everyone thought I was so dam 'hard
I never needed to fight.

As I said she gave it to Oxfam
It could of gone god knows where
Then one night when I was watching the news
I nearly fell off me chair

They were interviewing that Nelson Mandela
About some minor tribal dispute
They was all in their tribal regalia
Except some bastard wearing my suit.

He was wearing my shades out of Woolworth's
And he had my steel comb in his hand
And with only that as a weapon
He had won back his tribal home land.

And I just knew that tucked in his pocket
Was my partly used packet of three
But the thing that pissed me off most
He looked a bloody sight harder than me

AUSTRALIA'S REVENGE

We had this Aborigine move to our village
And we're glad he didn't stay
Christ he were a queer fellow
I mean strange I know he weren't gay

He was a big strapping lad with charisma
And had strange powers to make folks disappear
Well since old Mrs. Johnson caught religion
We aint had strange powers around here

He had this bag of old bones strung round his neck
And used to toss it down on the floor
And when he did it in front of a stranger
We never saw them round here no more

We had this Aborigine move to our village
We were glad when he went away
He dint mind his business like strangers should
He just had to have his own say

He used to come in the pub and drink other folk's beer
You daren't let go of your glass
Strangers would have a bit of a moan
We weren't scared but we let it pass

The woman folk all seemed to like him
They reckoned that he meant no harm
Even my wife stood up for the sod
She said he had got lots of charm

We don't like charm round here
It isn't natural in a in a bloke
Why couldn't he be like the rest of us
And ignore our wives when they spoke

We had this aborigine move to our village
For a time we thought he might stay
We used to hate it when he came in the pub
But the women thought him O.K

My wife said it were because I were jealous
Cos he winked at the women and that
Well that didn't bother me one little bit
Except they always seemed to wink back

The women took turns to do his cleaning
And supposedly cook him his tea
And I'm sure the young widow Wilson
Gave him things she used to give me

Then the women started to squabble
About who should do what on which day
And I think that my wife were one of them
Though she didn't actually say

It totally changed our small village
It didn't seem like the same place
All the men walking round looking grumpy
And my wife with a smile on her face

Then some of the men put their foot down
And made their womenfolk all stay at home

My wife said that were just churlish
Leaving him all on his own

It all came to a head on one Sunday
When the vicar put his pennyworth in
He pronounced during his service
That the women should be helping him

They'd stopped helping him in his garden
And no one were cleaning the church
Since the abo had moved to the village
He'd just been left in the lurch

The aborigine said he didn't mind
There were plenty of women to share
He were talking about our wives
And they didn't seem to care

We were all fed up with smiling women
Well that isn't how it should be
They should be moaning and miserable
And at home getting the tea.

Then he just disappeared into the night
Nobody knew where he went
There were tears in the eyes of some women
But it stopped their bloody descent

Now the vicar has got back is lackey's
And we've all got back our wives
And I hope he moves to Norwich
And buggers up their lives

They took turns to do his cleaning. And
supposedly cook him his tea.

MY WIFE'S LONG NIGHT OUT

My wife went to a night club
Didn't get back till next day,
Said she'd been abducted by aliens
Well it happens so what could I say

When I asked what they did to her
She said it weren't nice to tell
But she had this strange smile on her face
And kept humming and singing as well

Then she started calling out this name
At night when we were in bed
She said it were the aliens
But they don't have names like Ned

then something weird started to happen
And it really gave me a fright
Those aliens started abducting her
Every Saturday night

One night while she was out being abducted

She didn't come back and I don't understand

What would aliens want with her clothes and car

And my last couple of grand

My wife got abducted every Saturday night

We ran a pub in a small village in Suffolk for a few years in the late nineties and the early 2000s, it was a truly village pub with a public bar and a saloon. This is now a thing of the past but the public bar was used by the old original Locals and the saloon was used by most passing trade and the newcomers to the village.

The following poem was written for one of the newcomers who had decided he was going back up north which I found difficult to Understand. We had a few regulars from northern parts in our Suffolk pub for some reason, I suppose they come for the weather or the better looking women. I don't suppose we will ever know. We became quite good friends despite them calling me a southern Jesse an me calling them northern bastards. One of them decided to move back to Yorkshire resulting in the following goodbye poem. Although I don't normally apologise for my poems I will say that the views expressed in the following are good humored banter and I'm sure some of the north is quite nice,

ODE TO A NORTHERN GENTLEMAN

This chap from up the north arrived
And brightened up our lives
He shagged all our single women
Then tried it on our wives

There wasn't any malice in him
He didn't mean no harm
You had to smile as he seduced your wife
Well, he did it with such charm.

He were a northerner and a gentleman
Though that doesn't ring quite true,
But you sometimes saw his common side
When he had had a few.

He used to snog our women
He would never wait his turn,
And he spent more a week on Guinness
Than most of us could earn.

So goodbye northern bastard
You never did much wrong
But Suffolk will be a safer place
When you're back where you belong.

Get back up there amongst dry stone walls
And the coal dust and the grime
To the land of ugly women
Where it's raining all the time

Get back amongst them dark black hills
Where us Jesse's fear to go
Where its two foot deep in sheep shit
And there's soot mixed with the snow

Piss off northern bastard
To your horrible gnat's piss beer
But call and see us any time
If you're ever back round here

SYMPATHY FOR AN AGEING LOVER

It must be worse for you; you used to be a beauty.
It must be hard, now your looks are gone
Time has took its toll, and you're starting to look old
And your breasts that once were large are now just long.

It must be worse for you, once you were gorgeous.
Men often used to stop and stare,
Now your hands are gnarled a bit, and your skin
don't quite fit.
And time has been and bugger'd up your hair.

It must be worse for you, once you were stunning.
I remember when you were tall and sleek'
You try to keep alive the dream, with the use of
Nivea cream,
But a month's supply now just lasts a week.

It must be worse for you once you were lovely.
Now your reflection is not what you want to see,
It must really hurt, now you've nothing left that's pert,
And now your lovely chin has turned to three.

It must be worse for you, once you were a beauty.

I remember how you used to be,

It must be really hard, now your hips have turned
to lard,

It's worse for you, but it isn't much fun for me.

I DON'T MIND GETTING OLD

I'm thinking of buying a vest.

I've reached that time of life.

When I can slurp, drinking a cup of tea.

And eat peas off of my knife.

I can start being rude to children.

And I'm learning to cough and spit.

I'm really quit looking forward.

To being a doddery old gitt.

I'll grow a yellow moustache.

And force me grand kids to give me a kiss.

And I'll buy a pair of them trousers

That always smell of piss.

I'll bump into people in the street.
And hit them with me brolly.
And when they turn and look at me.
I will look frail and they'll say sorry.

I can buy a plastic shopping bag.
And let the handles fray.
And drink mild and bitter.
And moan if have to pay.

I'll lose control of me bladder.
And get one of them bags instead.
So when I've had ten pints at night.
I don't have to get out of bed.

So I'm going to be a doddery old gitt.
Just as soon as I can.
Or failing that I've half a mind
To be a dirty old man.

MY FAVOURITE WOMAN

She sits beside me with her head upon my knee

And gives me such a loving look when she looks
up at me

She does everything I ask of her without a single moan

And never makes me talk to her when I want to be alone

She excepts just what I give her never asks for more

And she's always pleased to see me when I walk
in the door

She is better than any woman I have ever had before

Everyone should have a Golden Labrador.

THE UNFORTUNATE ACCIDENT

I had drunk too many beers and had to go to the loo

When I got my Willie out it looked like I had two

But I put the wrong one away

And pissed all over my shoe

PRUE'S NEW MAN

Prue were having a problem getting men into her
bed

So she bought herself a rubber one and loved him so
she said

He did everything she asked him and never farted
(now, there's a perk)

He is the perfect husband except he won't get up
for work

THE RISE AND FALL OF MRS. JOHNSON

During the war old Mrs. Johnson
Well she was young Mrs. Johnson then,
Caught this terrible dose of religion
And began praying for all our young men.

Her husband was out in the desert
Amongst all the bullets and shit,
So I suppose it wasn't surprising
That she wanted to do her bit.

She started helping out our young vicar
And visited him every day,
She was always the first one down on her knees
When he said let us pray.

Well her husband stayed out in the desert
For a year or maybe two,
And she carried on with her good works
Well it gave her something to do.

Until one day right out of the blue
At the bishop's grand reception,
She announced bold as brass
That she had had an immaculate conception.

She had been visited by the lord she said
She was the chosen one,
And in a month or two
She would have the good lord's son.

Well there were talk that she'd be canonized
And made in to a saint,
Our church became quite famous
And got a lick of paint.

People came from miles' around
Just to look at her,
There were even talk of three wise men
Called Frank Incense and Myrrh.

The people from the wireless came
And all of the worlds press
She had her picture in the daily sketch
Serene in a long white dress.

Her husband didn't come back from the war
Like we all said he might,
Well them Germans was still being a nuisance
And someone had to fight.

Then one day in June she gave birth
And it really shook the world,
When the holly infant it were born
It was a ginger headed girl.

Well the vicar said it was an omen
Cos he were ginger too,
But there were an awful lot of doubters
And a hell of a to do.

The messiah grew up to be a barmaid,
And travels round to hide her shame,
But you will know her if you meet her,
Jesus Johnson is her name.

<u>Jesus Johnson</u>

I AINT JEALOUS

That Peter Stringfellow were in the paper to day

Telling how he pulls them gorgeous birds

It's all down to is well kept body and good looks

And all is fancy words

It's nothing to do with his money' fast cars'

And big fancy night club

It's nice to know he could pull birds like that

If he ran a village pub

BAD TIMES

I met this dirty woman once
And I can't get it from my head
There was a cheese grater and some rubber gloves
Hid beneath the bed
She was wearing leather panties
And her bra was made of steel
And she had eight inch stilettos
And made me suck the heel
She got out a cat of nine tails
And a studded leather belt
And she gently smacked me with it
And asked me how it felt
She made me tie her to the bed
So she could not get away
Then she said now get your clothes off
It's time for us to play
She said pass the cheese grater
I'm gone to give your bits a rub
Scared the bloody life from me
So I ran back to the pub.

MY OLD DAD

My old dad earned a shilling a week
And lived in a shed on the farm
He had a cockerel tied to the leg of the bed
Cos he couldn't afford an alarm.

He were up at five, seven days a week
Whatever the weather were like
And walked three miles to the cow shed
Cos he couldn't afford a bike.

Then he'd milk fifty cows by hand
And could name them just like that
He wore a knotted hankie on his head
Cos he couldn't afford a hat.

He'd get home from work at nine o'clock
With a rabbit in each hand
And he'd still go out in the garden
And dig is bit of land.

Well he worked bloody hard all is life
Just to put food into the pot.
And what has he got to show for it
Bloody arthritis, that's all he's got

WHY ARE SUSPENDERS SO NICE

When I first noticed things were wrong
I denied it that can't be rite
But there were several times
When it kept me awake at night

You see Id spent lots o. time in the kitchen
Cooking and cleaning and stuff
And I found myself a worrying
Cos me hands was getting rough

Well I suppose that's quite natural
There's nothing wrong you'll say
Except I started buying Nivea
And that oil of bloody Olay

Still I kept on doing my womanly chores
Like the ironing and washing up
Then I discarded my favorite mug
And bought a bone china cup

Then I decided to buy some marigolds
To keep beside the sink
There were loads of colors to choose from
But I ended up buying pink

Then I got interested in interior design
And pastel color effects
And wanted women for their company
And not just occasional sex

Then shopping got a pleasure
And clothes were hard to choose
And I stated visiting shoe shops
Just to try on shoes

Then I started to get real tetchy
Once a month about full moon
And really stated worrying
I'd start menstruating soon

I were reading woman's realm
And listening to housewife's choice
And even stated talking
In a winging high pinched voice

Well that were bad enough
But then to cap it all
I could see my mouth getting bigger
And feel my brain getting small

It were worrying enough
When I thought I were tuning gay
But I were changing to a woman
More and more each day

So I bought myself a pipe
And grew a bushy beard
In the hope no one would notice
That I was acting weird

I started drinking pints of beer
And went to football with the guy's
But I couldn't help but notice
How the player's had nice thighs

Then one night while I was knitting
In front of the T.V
I saw this documentary
About that H.R.T

Well the wife she were on it
And I really don't know why
But it were making her look younger
So I thought that I would try

So I used to pinch a couple
Every now and then
It don't say on the packet
That they don't work on men

Well since I came off the H.R.T
Most of the symptoms have gone
Except I gets this occasional impulse
To put suspenders on.

Quiet night in

RONO

There was a time when it didn't matter
We'd just run and play in the wood
The summer holiday lasted for ever
And life was happy and good

Then you had to start wearing long trousers
Cos your mum said you'd soon be a man
And life was no longer just one big game
And you were told you must have a plan

You had to study when you went to school
Else you wouldn't get the right job
Old Rono was held up as example
Of how you could soon be a slob

He was the local ne'er-do-well
Never worked a day in his life
He just lived down the road in a council house
With loads of kids and his wife

He used to sit on his step rolling fags
And drinking from a bottle of beer
He used to shout and swear an awful lot
If anyone came near

My mum wanted me to be
Like the man that lived next door
He drove a big shiny red rover
And only worked nine till four.

Old Rono never had a car
And never got up till one
But he was always laughing and drinking beer
And always seemed to have fun

The man next door used to worry a lot
And his wife was a sour faced bat
Rono used to laugh and sing
And play with his kids and that.

So I wasted the end of my childhood
And struggled to get a good job
And Rono still sits on his step
Rolling fags and drinking beer like a slob

Now I have got a red rover
And a mortgage till I'm sixty-three
And Rono still sits there on his step
And I recon he's laughing at me

Old Rono

THAT'S MY BOY

I got this girl in the family way
When I was just a lad
And we were told we must get married
By her brothers and her dad

"The child will get called a nasty name
If its born and you're not wed"
So being a bit of a coward
I did just what they said

So without delay we got married
Just like they said we should
And she gave birth to this nasty lad
who never was no good

he grew up to be a right little shite
and my marriage never lasted
the whole darn thing was a waste of time
because he still gets called a bastard.

THE ABBO'S RETURN

The door of the pub flew open
And in burst Slurpy Jack
He sprayed us as he told us
The bloody Abbo's back

Past readers will probably remember
The trouble he caused in our lives
What with his scrounging and his lying
Not mention his effect on our wife's

He just upped and moved up to Norwich
At least that's what was said
But some of the chaps were so bitter
They secretly hoped he was dead

He'd lived in an old railway carriage
Left from Doc Beaching's day
When he buggerd up our railways
And took our branch line away

Slurpy had an allotment
Down by the old railway line
And the Abbo had pissed on his rhubarb
Cos' he refused to make him some wine

We decided to set up a posse
A gang or even a mob
The village copper didn't want to know
Said it wasn't his job.

We gathered the lads all together
To run the basted from town
He promised he'd be no more trouble
He'd come back to settle down

There wasn't a man among us
That believed what the lying sod say
But some women folk ad followed us
And insisted we let him stay

So for now it must be a stalemate
The womenfolk must be obeyed
But we won't let him get the better of us
His eviction is just delayed

THE WET DREAM

I were stranded on this life raft
The sea were wild and high
Joanna Lumley she were there
There were only her and I

The sea she were a raging
There were water every where
But she still looked bloody sexy
With a fish stuck in her hair

The raft were being tossed and turned
By the mighty sea
I held her to stop her coming off
And she did her best for me

Then a mighty wave struck our raft
And split it at the seams
Marry me if we get home she cried
I do like them wet dreams

CRYING MAKES YOUR NOSE RUN

She was beautiful,
I admired her from afar for years
Even thinking about her now
Brings tears straight to my ears.

She had eyes like a baby cow
And legs from another dimension
And as she walked past me, as she always did
The air was filed with tension

I used to dream that she would just smile at me
Looking back now it seems a bit daft
Once I winked to get her attention
And she smiled and then she laughed

Once, I went to a party
And she was with some chap having fun
And that was when I first noticed
How crying can make your nose run

She worked in the same building as me
I used walk round hoping we would collide
She'd be laughing by the coffee machine
And I'd buy some to be by her side

She never even new I existed
Though I were always in her way
Trying to catch a whiff of her perfume
Thinking desperately of something to say

Then one day when I was lurking
Just watching the sun on her hair
And listening to the sensual rustle
As she moved about in her chair

She turned and smiled
Hallo my name's Jane she sexily sighed
My chance ad come I looked cool
AH AH ER, I replied

I couldn't believe it, my tongue
Felt ten times its natural size
I could feel the tears in my ears
And see the wax in me eyes

I could smell the sweat on me forehead
And my arm pits went all dry
And I collapsed into a crumpled heap
And immediately started to cry

She never looked my way again
I didn't exist, not nor more
I'd ad my chance to talk to her
And ended up on the floor

That were over thirty years ago
And my confidence grew again
I recovered like young men do
But I still remember the pain

I saw her the other day
And she's still got eyes like a cow
And her legs are as long as they were then
Though you can see the veins in them now

And she smiled and she had a gap in her teeth
But her hair and her smell were the same
She spoke to me said she remembered my face
But couldn't remember my name

It all flooded back I couldn't reply
My ears misted up and there was wax in me eye
And my mouth was wet and my palms went dry
And I fell on the ground and started to cry

She walked away out of my life
perhaps for another thirty years
But I will always remember them cow like eyes
And it still brings tears to me ears

She had eyes like a baby cow

THE TROUBLE WE HAD WITH YEAST

Mr. Grimes what delivered the bread
Was a randy old sod of renown
He used to deliver the bread round our village
Though he did all is baking in town

He had lovely soft hands from all that kneading
And making dough to put in the bread
And the yeast that he used to rise it
Got in is blood so they said

All the women in the village bar one
At some time had been in his bed
But we'd all had his misses
So nothing were ever said

He set his sights on Mrs. Johnson
We reckoned she must be the last
We all called her the Madonna
Cos of things that occurred in the past

Well Mr. Johnson had been quite protective
Since he got back from the war
He reckoned people had taken advantage
And it wouldn't happen no more

Mr. Grimes saw that as a challenge
And he went to all sorts of pains
To get inside her affections
As the yeast surged through his veins

He tried very hard to seduce her
With is world famous meat pie's
But Mr. Johnson were always there watching
With jealousy green in his eyes

So he found him a job in his bake house
To keep him out of the way
And he took Mrs. Johnson French fancies
Two or three times every day

Well Mr. Johnson he were not stupid
Nor were he a violent man
But we knew he'd give Grimes his comeuppance
But we couldn't work out his plan

Our bread didn't come one Monday
But Mr. Johnson delivered next day
He said they'd had an over production
And he were giving meat pies away

They was the best we've ever tasted
And so big they was nearly a feast
They was nothing like we were used to
And the meat tasted slightly of yeast

The police sent a man down from London
To find out wear old Grimes had gone
Co-operation weren't very forthcoming
So he didn't stay round here for long

Grimes still comes up in our conversation
And we wonder if he's live or dead
But them meat pies never get mentioned
Well some things are best left unsaid.

The pie was so big it was almost feast

GROWING UP

They say I should grow up
But where is the fun in that
I like going out and getting pissed
And acting like a prat

I still like chasing women
Though I aint caught one for a wile
But when I go out kitted up
I often get a smile

I put on my fancy tie
That matches my fancy shirt
And go down the over sixties club
And have a little flirt

They got this new Viagra now
That keeps blokes my age more active
I only took it once
Cos it made the wife attractive.

I've got myself a motor bike
And keep myself in trim
And bought a fancy track suit
And hangs about the gym

But if I pulled a willing woman now
I don't think I would pounce
I'm stiff in almost every place
Except the place that counts,

THE BRACE

I 'were riding in Waltham on my bike when I
were only eight,
Going home for dinner and I thought I might
be late.
I pulled on the break far too hard and came to
sudden grief,
My bike reared up and threw me off and I
landed on me teeth

Our school dentist was a big old chap with
fingers like octopus legs
It really weren't much fun him messing with
your peg's
His breath smelt just like garlic, like most
dentist's do
And hanging off the end of his nose were a
little drop of dew

He pulled the stump from me broken tooth
and left a great big hole

There was room for a fence post or perhaps a
telegraph pole

He rummaged in a cardboard box for
something to fill the gap

It was full of broken dentures and all sorts of
other crap.

He came up with this silver tooth that were too
big for my gob

But it had a London hall mark and he said it
would do the job

It had a couple dents in, and much to my
dismay

It dazzled folks when I smiled at them and
they had to look away

The dam thing kept falling out, so to hold it in
its place

My dad got some old paper clips and made
mettle brace

I dared not even kiss a girl till I was
seventeen

Then my brace got caught on Julie's lip you
should of heard her scream

The fire brigade was called to cut us both
apart

She never spoke to me again it broke my
teenage heart

Even now that I'm all grown up the vision is
still there

Of a coughed one day that left my tooth
hanging in some girl's hair.

But I got through my adolescence as metal
mouth the clown

The other kids all laughed at me but it never got
me down

I never used to worry when the other kids
laughing all the time

Cos my tooth were a perfect aerial and it were
tuned to Caroline.

THE SPORT OF PRINCESSES

I never really saw the point
Of playing all them silly sports
but each to their own
I suppose it takes all sorts

They say you can make a living
As a footballer or a jockey
But I can't understand why grown men
Play bloody hockey

Rugby players sing and swear
And laugh at each other's farts
But grown playing hockey
What a bunch of tarts

Football players earn big money
And get to chat up all the birds
But grown men waving hockey sticks
What a bunch of nerds

They prance about in all the mud

In any kind of weather

It can't be the game they like

They just like to bath together

Sport of Princesses

A CHRISTMAS STORY

I got back early from the night shift
And found soot all in the hearth
So I had to sweep the bugger up
Before I could have me bath.

Then what did I discover
Soot all up the stair
And a red and white fur uniform
Tossed on the landing chair.

I peeped into the bedroom
And there was Santa clause
He were completely naked
And my wife didn't have no draws

I'm afraid I lost my temper
And smacked Santa on the nose
He ran and sniggered ho ho ho
As he gathered up his clothes,

When she'd asked for Christmas money
Screw Santa is what I said
So apparently it's my fault
I found him in my bed.

GOOD DEAL

I lent my new bucket to my neighbor
And he never gave it back
Denied he ever had it
Said piss off just like that

Well they say revenge is sweet
And I believed that all my life
But I aint never had such sweet revenge
As shagging my neighbor's wife

LET'S START A SECT

Frank turned all religious,
Said he'd been blessed by real holy water.
Turns out he'd been given a golden shower
By the local vicar's daughter.

THE CELEBRITY

When he first came in the pub
They say watch him he's famous
I thought that's nice he's welcome here
They dint say he were famous, for drinking
other people's beer

TIME TO GIVE UP

I aint quite old enough to be a dirty old man
I'll have to wait a while for that
And I'm past the age to be a super stud
and anyway I'm too fat

But I met this lady of ninety-five
and they calls her nifty Lille
and I know 'cos she told me
she's sexually active still

So I thought I'd be her toy boy
I'd found my niche at last
but when I tried to catch her
she ran too bloody fast

I'd buy her double whiskeys
to try and slow her down
but I'd be far too drunk to stand
and she'd buy another round

I tried real hard to impress her
with my good looks and my wit
and I'd do a couple of press-ups
to show that I was fit

But she'd still run rings around me
make me feel six inches tall
she convinced me I'm too old
to be a toy boy after all.

SMART MOVE RONNY

I 'aint never met a man from London

That didn't know Ronnie Cray

He were a lovely bloke

If you believe all the things, they say

But if he were so clever

Now he's done his porridge

Why did he decided to end his days?

In a boring place like Norwich

THE SINGER

I was listening to this blues singer
Christ he had a hard life
There always seemed to be someone
Messing with his wife

He'd spend all his day
Working in the red hot sun
Then he'd work all night
While others were having fun

One day his kids were gone
Then his dog was dead
He picked cotton over near Dunmow
Till his fingers fairly bled

He'd lived in a cardboard box
With nothing at all to eat
And huddled around a candle
As his only source of heat

He'd walked a hundred miles for a woman
Just find she had gone
He'd had some bloody bad luck
And never had no fun

Well I reckon that must have been in the past
But I really don't know how
He's only twenty-six
And he's a history teacher now

A BIG PERSONALITY

We had this kid in oure class at school

They called him Donkey Bligh

The older girls loved to play with him

I never did know why.

THE UNIDENTIFIED OBJECT

I found this thing in my wife's top draw
The kind of thing I aint seen before
So I took it down and shew old Jim
He had to admit it puzzled him

So we took it along and shew old Mr. Hall
He works for the gas board so he knows it all
He says I don't know what the bugger be
I'd ask the wife, if it were me.

Well I dint want her to know I'd been in her draw
So I just put it back and said no more

Then the antiques road show came to town
I thought I'll take my wife's thing down
I Shew it to this so called expert
He was naught but a lad

When I got my wife's thing out he went bloody mad
Got these two men to show me the door
Told me never come back no moor
And I still don't know what the bloody things for

We took it along to show old Mr. Hall

HE'S OUT THERE

He's built like a brick shit house
And he acts just like one too
And I bet he likes to beat his wife
When he's had a few.

He's nastier than a scrap yard dog
Through and through he's bad
Even his mum don't like him
And he never knew his dad.

He used to pull little girls hair
When they came out to play
And I reckon when he were circumcised
They threw the wrong bit away.

His breath stinks and he's got bad teeth
And he hasn't got a friend
He will die of a painful illness
Or come to a violent end.

He's never had a woman
In all his rotten life
He has sex on his own
And is underpants are rife.

You can tell all that from his hand writing
if you study it and take your time
As you sit down and write your cheque
To pay your parking fine.

CHIP OFF THE OLD BLOCK

I felt I needed a Hero

When I were just a lad

So I suppose it isn't surprising

My hero was my dad.

So I started smoking woodbines

Farting and drinking beer

They didn't like that much at primary school

Isn't life bloody queer?

The following was written again all in one go in a matter of minutes with no alterations required, in response to a request from some of the members of our local folk club, for a poem with chorus so everyone could join in as with most of the songs performed by various people. Again I have no recollection of ever meeting or hearing about a chap with this problem, named Jack or otherwise. I have probably read it a 100 times to an audience and it always goes down well and the punch line still makes me laugh out loud even now

JACK'S GREAT LOSS

Jack came in the pub one night,
With a tear in his eye,
He were about to lose his two oldest friends
And it were hard to say goodbye.

Ever since he could remember
He had scratched them every day
Now they was riddled with something horrible
And he was having them taken away

Goodbye old friend, so long old friend, you never
did quite match
But what will I do in the mornings, without you
to rub and scratch

One had gone all horrible
And was covered in Tick's and fleas,
The other was black and mangy
And riddled with disease.

So he went to see an expert
And got them out on show
He just poked them with a pencil
And said sorry, they'll have to go.

Goodbye old friend, so long old friend, you never
did quite match
But what will I do in the mornings, without you
to rub and scratch

So he scratched one every morning
To try and kill the fleas
And the other he rubbed with ointment
To rid it of disease.

But the therapy wasn't working
That became quite clear
He was going to have to lose them
And the day was drawing near.

Goodbye old friend, so long old friend, you
never did quite match
But what will I do in the mornings, without you
to rub and scratch

None of us had seen them
Cos he kept them out of sight
Except sometimes for his wife's amusement
He would get them out at night.

We tried real hard not to take the piss
But we started to run a book
To see if he could be persuaded
To let us have a look.

Goodbye old friend, so long old friend, you never
did quite match
But what will I do in the mornings, without you
to rub and scratch

We tried really hard not laugh
At the pore old buggers plight
But we persuaded him to show us all
In the pub next Saturday night.

The pub were packed to the gunwale's
When Saturday came around,
And Jack walked in with a tear in both eyes
Nobody made a sound.

Goodbye old friend, so long old friend, you
never did quite match
But what will I do in the mornings, without you
to rub and scratch

Jack stood up on a chair
The women all backed away

And he gave us a look, that said don't laugh
And got them out on display.

Well I have always been a fair man
And I judge things on their merits
But it seemed it were all too much fuss
Over a couple of knackered Ferrets

Goodbye old friend, so long old friend, you never
did quite match
But what will I do in the mornings, without you
to rub and scratch

Please try not to cry

A chap called John Low walked in our pub one night and asked if he could play our piano, He was accompanied by 2 jack Russell's and a lovely wife, he sat at the piano with a dog either side of him on the piano stool and blew us away. I can't remember what he played that first time I just remember we loved it. He told me a few lies and I told him some back, and we became friends and this poem was written as a response to his stories as was the poem "the brace"

THE ICE CREAM BOY

When I was a boy, it was my joy,
To play on Martlsham heath,
My dog and me, we were free,
No grownups to give us grief

One sunny day, I was off to play,
But my dad spoiled my scheme
We couldn't go free, he needed me,
To sell his blooming ice cream.

Not in the park, but in the dark,
Down at the old flea pit,
I looked a prat, in his silly hat,
And a white coat that didn't fit.

Dam great queue, what could I do,
Where do I begin?
Seventeen P, what's that for three,
Panics setting in.

Feeling strange, can't work out the change,
Don't know what to do,
Panicking now, sweat on me brow,
School friends in the queue

Film restarts, a couple of tarts,
Start to take the piss,
I can't see, I need a pee,
Must get out of this.

Tear in my eye, mustn't cry,
Couldn't stand the shame,
Drop to floor, crawl to the door,
Dad screaming out my name.

Back in the sun, start to run,
Bit between my teeth,
Now I'm free, I must be,
Back on Martlsham heath.

There is nowhere else quite like it, when I want to
fell free
Out on Martlesham heath, just my dog and me.

Not too fussy

I like my women skinny
And I like em fat
Not so fat of course t
So there's bits you can't get at

Good deal

I went to a wife swapping party
They were all the rage at the time
The others all got a woman for there's
I got three cans of larger for mine

Hard life

Who said life begins at forty
They must be bloody mad
Arthritis begins at forty
Just ask my poor old dad

MY HERO

During the war my old granddad

Killed one hundred Germans one day

And when the Italians heard he were coming

The buggers all ran away

He blew up a bridge with only one fart

And stopped a doodle bug hitting the ground

So why is it when grandma's asleep?

He's frightened to make a sound

When the Italians heard he was coming they
turned and ran away

DON'T WORRY ABOUT ME

Thanks for asking
I feel much better now
I got through another week
I really don't know how.

Thanks very much for asking
The old troubles back again
I'm not one to talk about it
I'm no stranger to pain.

The doctor says my prostrate
Is a miracle to behold
But I'm not one to complain
I know I won't grow old

But thanks for asking
Now it's just pill after pill
But you'll never hear me moan
Even though I'm always ill.

I suppose I shall struggle on
Until the bitter end
I don't mind the pain
Me and pain are like old friends

Me hemorrhoids don't bleed as much
As they used to do
I'm still a martyr to arthritis
And I've just had Asian flue

The doctor says I've got a syndrome
I dint quite catch its name
And it doesn't really hurt that much
It's just one extra pain.

I know I've got some illnesses
I haven't yet been told
Just look inside my hanky
How's that for a cold

You don't have to worry about me
I'll probably be all right
As long as I take me tablets
I'll probably last the night but thanks for asking
I'll survive I'm sure
But I just can't understand
Why no one asks no more.

MR. SINGS REVENGE

If ever you are hungry,
And need sustenance in a hurry,
I can thoroughly recommend
Mr. Sings number two meat curry.

It's got onions and Garlic,
An unspecified sort of meat,
Lots of secret ingredients,
That are wonderful to eat.

It brings sweat onto your forehead,
And makes your lips go numb,
And you rush into the toilet
As it burns out of your bum,

And when it splatters on the porcelain,
It's a wonder to be seen,
As it burns off all the lime scale
And leaves it squeaky clean.

Although it fascinating to watch,
You must flush it straight away,
I watched for too long once,
And it set as hard as clay.

And as it pops and hisses,

On its way out to sea,
You wonder what would happen,
If you tried curry number three.

ALL I EVER WANTED WAS BE A BLUE'S SINGER

It's bloody hard for an Essex boy to learn to sing
the blues

I aint never picked no Cotton, or gone to work without no
shoes.

I've never had a dog that's died or a woman that
has gone

I aint never had the blues so bad I just can't carry on.

I aint never tasted grits or even seen a black eyed pea

And working on a chain gang means bugger all to me.

I aint never drunk no bourbon till me heads about
to split

I had some abbot ale once but that just made me shit

I aint never had a wicked woman that made me
really sad

I had a really fat one once but even that weren't bad.

I aint never been to prison done bird porridge or time

Well I never had the reason to go and do the crime.

But I'd go through all that crap if I had the chance to choose

And if I thought that it would help me learn to sing the blues

All I ever wanted was to learn to sing the blues

THE SKULL

I found this skull on my allotment
While digging in the ground
So I biked down to the police house
To show him what I'd found.

Well it sent him all a fluster
He didn't know what to do
So he called his chief inspector
There were hell of a to do.

They sent a man from Scotland Yard
To investigate the crime,
Well it must of happened years ago
So it seemed a waste of time.

They cordoned off the allotments
And erected loads of lights,
Then they poked around with plastic sticks
For several days and nights.

There was some speculation
From folks that live round here
That it could be Grimes the Baker
Who disappeared last year.

The scull were sent to London
Where the clever buggers live,
And they had the right equipment
To check the skull out with.

The forensic expert's looked at it
And made a big to do,
But as is often the case with expert's
They hadn't got a clue.

The cleaner picked it up
'cos tidiness were her pride,
And it were her that first noticed
There were something writ inside.

It says made in Stratford
That's somewhere up near Warwick
It even had his name in
I think his name was Yorick.

AMNESIA

Sometimes when I've had a few

I likes to sit and think

But I can't remember what I thinks about

I recon that's the drink.

THE MORON

No one would give him time of day

If he walked past they looked the other way

Everyone said don't you trust that man

And all he'd done was drink Guinness strait from
the can

THE TREE

I bought one of them bonsai trees

I watered it every day

It took three years to grow an inch

So I threw the dam thing away.

AINT LIFE A BLOODY WORRY

Aint life a bloody worry their seems no end to it.
What with the Chinese building our power stations
And all that euro shit
And all them foreign people coming from god
knows where
It's all so bloody scary, it's not that I don't care

Where shall we hide our money now we can't trust
the bank
No one wants to take the blame so who we got to
thank
That bloody Angela Myrtle worries me to death
If that E U gets its way, we'll have nothing left
There are guns on the streets of London although I
never go
But it's less than 50 miles away that's why I
worry so
They say the globe is warming that's why we get too
much rain
And that's another thing where no one takes the
blame
I want to go on holiday but there's nowhere safe
to go
The places that seem quite safe are always full of
snow
They say you will have a heart attack if you put
sugar in your tea
Everything does you harm, that's how it seems to
me
The youngsters can't do sex now cos all of the
disease
And because of all the pesticides we soon won't
have no bees
We are losing all our native trees; we can blame
that on the Dutch

I know they will grow back again but it worries me
so much
Now I haven't been ill a day in my life but I've
wrote my epitaph
It say poor old Roger worried to death by the daily
Telegraph.

ESSEX MOUNTAIN RESCUE CLUB

My Mrs didn't like me going out
specially to the pub
Well I aint one for staying in
So I thought I'd join a club.

The saffron Walden power saw club
Had long since petered   out
After its good intentions
Had been put in serious doubt

So I was at a loose end
I started looking round
To see what I could join
But nothing could be found

So me and Mr Hall had a bright idea
We would start one of our own
Think of something our wives couldn't do
So we could get out alone.

It would have to be for the community
So our women folk couldn't moan
If we were out doing good
While they just sat at home

I was walking up Danbury hill
On my way up to the pub
When it struck me we could start
The Essex branch of the mountain rescue club.

Mr Hall thought it was a great idea
And we signed up straight away
Our wives were none too happy
But there wasn't much that they could say.

We have over thirty member's now
And we didn't even try
But if you get stranded on Danbury hill
We are all in the pub standing by.

THE UNMARKED VAN

You will say you can't remember
But I bet a pound you can
Being followed when you're in your car
By a big white unmarked van.

You look up in your mirror
And suddenly it's there
Any time of day or night
The bugger's everywhere.

Now I worry about silly things
Like the Chinese and heart attacks
But them vans are really sinister
I wonder what's in the back.

Perhaps they are under cover policemen
Or work for the K.G.B.
Or aliens checking out the planet
Surreptitiously.

Or they are stealing all the people
That mysteriously disappear
I read in the daily telegraph
It's hundreds every year.

Or are they just following you
To find out where you go
For some nefarious purpose
We will never know.

It may be just coincidence
And I'm just being a prat
I can't help but worry
I worry and that is that.

Now I've added to your burden
Pointing out that they are there
But why should I worry on my own
That would be unfair.

A MOEP

They say that I'm dyslexic

And I recon I've had enough

Even if I am dyslexic

I don't give a ckuf.

An embarrassing moment

I was making love to this pretty little thing

In a field behind a tree

Her mother crept up and caught us

And she said BAAH to me

Strange

I wonder about them moths

They come out when it's dark at night

Then they spend all their time

Hunting for the light.

MR BIG

I like it here in the village pub
And some strange folk come in here
Some come for the company
And some come for the beer.

But when the weather turns
And all the strangers are gone
That's when the real folk come in
And there's none as real as Ron.

They say he runs the Mafia
From his old folk's bungalow
And he only came to Essex
To keep his profile low.

They say he was a hoodlum
In his younger days
And he taught the business
To the Richardson's and Kray's.

He launders dirty money
In the village shop
And helps with the enquiries
Of the local village cop.

He used to deal in weapon's
And other dodgy stuff
He was mates with old Gadhafi
Till Ron got far too rough

They say he's fathered children
In almost every land
And no bad goes on round here
If Ron aint had a hand

He's got a sword inside his walking stick
And wears a collar for effect
And had his spine fused on purpose
To hide a shogun down his neck.

He planned the great train robbery
And stole millions from Brinks Matt
And they say he killed a stranger
For swearing at his cat

He's got the government in his pocket
And tells them what to do
And there's millions wiped off the stock
exchange
When big Ron's had a few

Now he's old they call him the vicar
And he's turned his hand to good
I don't think he was that bad
Just misunderstood.

THE SYNDROME

My doctor say's I've got a Syndrome

I can't remember which one it were

I went with a dirty woman once

Perhaps I caught it from her.

A LOAD OF CRAP

My crap house is down the garden
And I empty it in a pit
So why must I pay a sewage charge
So other folks can shit.

A FINAL THOUGHT

Life goes 0n they say
But that don't help a bit
That aint no consolation
If your life is full of shit

Lightning Source UK Ltd.
Milton Keynes UK
UKOW04f0954090316

269877UK00003B/30/P